The Naming of Names

Shash Trevett is a poet and a translator of Tamil poetry into English. Her poetry has appeared in many journals and anthologies, she has read widely across the U.K and internationally and is a winner of a Northern Writers' Award. Her pamphlet *From a Borrowed Land* was published in May 2021 by Smith|Doorstop. *Out of Sri Lanka: Tamil, Sinhala and English Poetry from Sri Lanka and its Diasporas* (Bloodaxe 2023, Penguin India 2023) which she co-edited with Vidyan Ravinthiran and Seni Seneviratne, was a Poetry Book Society Special Recommendation and one of the *Times Literary Supplement*'s Books of the Year for 2023.

The Naming of Names

Shash Trevett

smith|doorstop

the poetry business

Published 2024
by The Poetry Business
Campo House,
54 Campo Lane,
Sheffield S1 2EG
www.poetrybusiness.co.uk

Designed & typeset by Utter.
Printed by Imprint Digital

British Library Cataloguing-in-Publication Data.
A catalogue record for this book is available from the British Library.

Smith|Doorstop is a member of Inpress
www.inpressbooks.co.uk.

Distributed by BookSource, 50 Cambuslang Road,
Cambuslang Investment Park, Glasgow G32 8NB.

The Poetry Business gratefully acknowledges the support
of Arts Council England.

Contents

II

III

IV

For Kit & Becky

Dear Reader,

This book is filled with names. They will be strange
and unfamiliar to you. As you turn these pages you will be tempted
to gloss over, skim, even ignore them. Please don't. There is music
in these names.

Each is a whisper of a life lived and loved. Each a Tamil man,
woman or child killed by the state. Each a forgotten victim, mere
collateral damage, peripheral, expendable.

These names are mausoleums for those denied gravestones.
They are the staccatoed prayers of remembrance.
The hiss of incense on a funeral pyre.

Black July

I. Colombo 29 July 1983

Those were days of conflagration.
The Bristol building was burnt. So too
the Ambal Café. Sarathas, an emporium
on York Street, soon followed. So too
the shops on Baillie Street. Every Tamil business
in the Fort Area smouldered that July.
A Colombo engulfed in flames, as if Hanuman
was visiting Lankadeepa once again.

II. Welikade Prison, 25 July 1983

Knowing death would claim them there
Selvarajah Yogachandran, MP,
and Ganeshanathan Jeganathan, journalist,
willed their eyes to the Tamil blind
so that one day they might still look
on a free Tamil Eelam.

The mob gouged out their eyes first
that day in Welikade Prison.
They drank their blood and shouted:
Look, we have drunk the blood
of blinded Damila Demons.

Black July 1983 was the week-long pogrom of violence by Sinhala mobs against
Tamil civilians in the streets of Colombo. By the end of the week more than 2,000
Tamils would be murdered, 150,000 made homeless, and Sri Lanka would be
plunged into a civil war which would last twenty-six years.

His Name was Aasirvaatham

In the days after he was killed, his family
walked through rooms where sleep had forgotten
how to dream. Where moonlight whispered
with the tenderness of a sparrow's call.
They buried him under the tamarind tree.
Now, twenty years later, purple bougainvillea
all root and thorn, runs wild over his grave,
and his family turn over stones in my memory.

His name was Aasirvaatham, a blessing.
A name so Christian in Tamil. The aasirvaatham
of God a favourite among hymn writers.
Isn't it strange that this name, muscular
in sound in Tamil, is so feminine in English?
His name was Aasirvaatham, or Blessing.

Curiosities

Billie sang of Southern trees
but strange too are the ones growing
in the gardens around Jaffna.

Body parts protrude from mango, neem
or guava trees. A leg here, an arm there.
Etched on these are fragments of names:
Sinna....., *Path.....*, *or .....ini.*
Other trees bear eyes which play
within their whites silent films
of final moments. A knife, a gun, a penis.

If you are lucky, you can match
two legs or hands to make a whole.
Sinnathamby, a man or just a boy.
.....ini could be Ranjini, Priyatharsini,
or even Jeyapalini. A jigsaw
of possible pairings; names yearning
for completion.

The earth, angered by the lifting of her skirt
to bury body after body, claims these
as her own. Inkblots which do not wash away
in the rain. Tamil trees bear the most curious burdens.
The Sri Lankan Army the most unlikely of gardeners.

The Naming of Names 1

Abdulkathar	Abirami	Agilanathan	Ajanthan
Alagamma	Alaganayagam	Alagathurai	Alam
Amalathas	Amalaviji	Amalotpavarani	Ambalavanar
Ambikaipalan	Ameer	Amirtha	Amlini
Ananthapairavi	Aneez	Annamalar	Annammal
Annasingam	Annathas	Anumanthu	Anupama
Appaiah	Apthulnaginar	Apthulrasak	Arasakone
Arasamma	Archimuthu	Ariyakuddy	Ariyam
Arjunan	Arokianathan	Arooran	Artham
Arthanageswari	Arudkumaran	Arul	Arulamma
Arulthevarasa	Arumathurai	Arumugam	Arunananthi
Appulmajithu	Asilthas	Athiarunasalam	Atputharasa
Atputhavadivel	Aththappillai	Athukunchu	Babu
Balachandramurthy	Balakrishnan	Balananthan	Bararayasingam
Baviluppillai	Chakravarthi	Chandra	Chandran
Chithravadivel	Dasan	Dayalan	Dayalini
Dayaska	Dharmika	Dharsika	Dusintha
Eelan	Ekamparam	Elayavan	Fairuz
Faizal	Farook	Gajendran	Ganesh
Ganga	Geethanathani	Gnanakaran	Gnanamma
Gnanenthiran	Gunanathagam	Gurukulasamy	Hamsudeen
Harshan	Hemachandran	Hindujan	Ilachsegar
Illangeswaran	Ilango	Illayaperumal	Ilayathamby
Indran	Indravathana	Innachchi	Inpam
Inpanathan	Inthiramohan	Iraippu	Irasu
Iyampillai	Iyathurai	Iyer	Jamuna
Janani	Janagan	Jaseelan	Jauffer
Javanaraj	Jawar	Jeevan	Jegan
Jeganathan	Jehananthan	Jenakanth	Jepamani
Jesuratnam	Jeyachandran	Jeyakanthan	Jeyakumar

Before The War Came

At six o'clock every night, we'd bolt
the windows shut and set fire
to neem leaves, smoking on hot coals
in the bedrooms of my grandfather's house.
Gathering us on the veranda
he would take his place and delve
into his hoarded stories and tales
and we'd listen. Slotting ourselves
into a land, a people, a family, a race
before the war came.

At home it was a coiled mosquito-ring.
A snake puffing into a pool of ash.
Lying on her bed I'd watch the glitter
of my mother in rich reds and threaded golds,
in sparkles of light fetched from a casket
I loved to delve into. My parents were content
in their own space, among a land, a people,
a family, a race. Inheritors and bequeathers
by right, before the war came.

Night Bombings

When they began, artificial suns
tore open the sky in flashes
of such power, we waited
for the universe to explode.
Among the noise, the rattle of windows,
the counting of breath-pauses
from one detonation to the next –
we became night crawlers. Inhabitants
of dark spaces which wrapped tight
around our throats and would not let us breathe.

I.P.K.F.

The Indian Peace Keeping Force.
Protectors of the powerless
defenders of the disenfranchised.

We threw garlands around their semi-automatics
strewed petals beneath their T-72s
and welcomed them with prasatham.

To a war-weary population
they were heroes –
our friends, the Indians.

Not for long.

When our garlands broke
and turned to a reddened slurry
beneath marching boots

we re-named them
the Innocent People Killing Force.

Stone Walls

I remember the day the tanks rolled up
and we hid in that narrow room at the back
of the house. The birds fell silent.
In a moment of stillness we heard quite clearly
ek, do, teen, fire. Over and over, each shout
followed by a thud, each thud followed
by the crash and splintering of our world.

Glass shattered, timber collapsed. Dust
and frass danced in the air as the ceilings
blushed hot. I remember, over the boom
of the tanks, the tinkling of the piano
struck by bullets which ricocheted
off doors and walls. Our hearts paused. Petrified.

It took an hour for the house to capitulate
in flames, so the neighbours said later,
when they found us hardened into a stone
stillness. Although we returned many times
down the years to that room – on that day,
in that year, when the tanks had done
their job and moved away, we emerged
two bodies deadened, numbed, walled in.

That was our tragedy.

Uduvil, Nightfall

As the night descends suddenly again,
floating over the scent of jasmine
something else, a smell

my body wants to run from.
In the heavy silence sheathing the land

a weaver bird hurries to its nest.
Houses are shuttered, showing no light.

On the empty street, black tar cools.

I am like a ghost hovering over
this vacuum of non-life.

It is 6pm – curfew has begun
in this vacuum of non-life.
I am like a ghost, hovering over

the empty street as black tar cools.
Houses are shuttered, showing no light.

A weaver bird hurries to its nest.

In the heavy silence sheathing the land
my body wants to run from
something else, a smell

floating over the scent of jasmine
as the night descends suddenly, again.

The Naming of Names 2

Alagesan, Arigaran, Jeyasangar, Gnaneswaran.
Nadesan, Nadaraja, Vaitheeswaran, Maheswaran.
Nagalingam, Kanagasabapathy, Koneswaran, Sivaharan.
Nadeswaran, Sambasivam, Jegatheeswaran, Sivakumaran.
Ketheeswaran, Sivagnanam, Sivanantham, Uruthiran.
Piranavan, Naguleswaran, Sathasivam, Kodeeswaran.
Sathiaseelan, Umasankar, Sivamani, Sivananthan.
Sivagnanasuntharam, Satheeswaran, Thayalan, Pramatheeswaran.

Alaguvel, Kandaiah, Sriskandaraja, Ananthan.
Kugan, Thanikasalam, Kumaravel, Palamurugan.
Murugesu, Sanmugam, Senthilvel, Kuganthan.
Singaravel, Murugan, Maniam, Sivakurunathan.
Sanmukasuntharam, Thirukumar, Velan, Thayakaran.
Saravanamuththu, Sanmugavel, Velmurugu, Sanmuganathan.

Kamaleswari, Kamalathevi, Annalaxmi, Sriluxsumi.

Aravinthan, Arigaran, Jeyaraman, Kamalanthan.
Kamaleswaran, Kishanthan, Ramesh, Srirangan.
Vaikunthavasan, Thamotharam, Raman, Sritharan.

Kanapathy, Ganasekaram, Ganesalingam, Gnanaganesan.
Thevakanesan, Vinayagamurthy, Ganesaratnam, Vigneswaran.
Ganesamurthy, Vinayakam, Kanapathipillai, Ganesananthan.

Govindan, Gopalapillai, Mohanathan, Muralitharan.
Gopalakrishnan, Krishnaruban, Nanthakumar, Rathakrishnan.
Kovinthasamy, Kishnam, Kovintharasa, Mugunthan.
Kovarthani, Gopinath, Krishnan, Krishnapalan.
Krishnagopal, Shyam, Krishnaraja, Savariyan.

21

Kalavathi, Komathi, Sivakowri, Maheswari.
Rameswari, Sailaya, Sivakami, Loganayaki.

Om Rakini, Om Niranjini, Om Vairavi, mother Durga.
Om Sarasvathi, Om Gangathevi, we lay them at your feet.

This poem was influenced by the *Sri Lalitha Sahasranamam Stothram* a Hindu religious hymn which lists the thousand names of the mother goddess, Lalitha Devi. I have borrowed the metre and (adapted) the rhyme scheme from this Sahasranamam to list the various names of Hindu Gods and Goddesses used by Tamil people to name their children. The verses list in order, names for Siva, Murugan, Lakshmi, Vishnu, Ganesan, Krishna and Parvathi. These names were a benediction from parent to child, a talisman for a full life. Here they remain, the names of the dead.

And on the Ceiling, a Lizard

When he told me he had a little sister
the same age as me, I imagined
safety. A link. I braided
words into a chain of connection.

When he told me that his sister's
favourite subject was science
I lied and said – Mine too –
testing that bond of words.

When he rested his gun against the wall
and told me to lie down.
When he placed a grenade by the pillow
and unbuckled his belt

I watched the dust motes hang
in the air and the lizard freeze
on the ceiling, and knew that words
had never had the power to save me.

In Memory 1
for Bim-Bo

After you died, people said your birth horoscope
had foretold your death at thirteen.

That morning you had a bullet in your shoulder.
We were more concerned with your mother

shot in the chest. And you slipped away.

Now when I think of you on the ground,
flies homing to the corners of your eyes –

you were too quiet. And the blood
you left behind when we lifted you

onto the tractor, had pooled so deep
it took us three days to wash it away.

Three days after you turned thirteen
you were gone.

Her Name Was Thulasi

When she was born her parents named her Thulasi,
after the plant. (In English it is called Holy Basil).
She was their threshold between heaven and earth.

When she was shot, they made a paste
of thulasi leaves and tried to knit together
her body, to tether her spirit to themselves.

When she died Ganga reclaimed her,
scattering her essence among the leaves
and roots of their thulasi plant.

Her name was Thulasi, the keystone of their hearth.

At Jaffna Teaching Hospital, 21ˢᵗ October 1987

1.

They found them in the X-Ray Block.
Dr Sivapathasundaram, Consultant Paediatrician;
Dr Ganesharatnam, Surgical Registrar;
along with nurses Mankayarkkarasi,
Paramananthan, Leelawathy,
Sivapakiam and Ramanathan.

The Groundsmen Sukumar, Uruthiran,
Sivaloganathan and Varatharaja;
John Peter, Markandu, and Thurairaja;
Sivaraja and Yoganathan,
along with lab technician Ratnaraja,
were found together in the Overseer's Office.

Matron Vadivel and Shanmugalingam,
the Ambulance Driver, were there too.
The bodies of the two Overseers,
Krishnaraja and Selvaraja,
were found in the X-Ray Block.

Dr Parimelalakar (Outpatients' Department)
was found at the Clock Tower Road entrance.
Mr Vetharaniam outside Ward 12, in the corridor.
It is not clear where the body of Kanagalingam,
the Telephone Operator, was found.

2.

The Indian Army came along the corridors
firing. They fired into the Overseer's Office.

We lay among the dead bodies all through
the night as the soldiers did not leave.

One of the overseers had a cough
and a soldier threw a grenade at him.
He died, along with some others around him.
I know the Ambulance Driver died too.

A patient, unable to bear the tension,
got up with his hands in the air, crying
"We are innocent. We support Indira Gandhi".
They threw a grenade at him.

3.

Dr Ganeshamurthy, interviewed
on the 20th anniversary, still remembered
the smell of blood pooling
on the floor of the hospital.

4.

The staff evacuated everyone from Ward 8
and we rushed to the X-Ray Block.
We crowded into one room.
Then the soldiers arrived.
They threw grenades into the room
and sprayed it with gunfire.
People were screaming, falling
on top of each other.

I felt a stabbing pain in my leg
and collapsed. Others fell on top of me.

5.

8.30am the next morning.
Dr Sivapathasuntheram was shot.

Dr Sivapathasuntheram, the Paediatrician,
who had not been present at the massacre
was returning from the mortuary,
with two nurses, when he was shot.

I heard Dr Sivapathasuntheram's voice.
He was shouting: "We are doctors,
we are nurses. We are innocent."
A soldier standing on the stairs
took aim and shot him. Repeatedly.
Later we learnt he had shielded
the nurses on either side of him.
They survived.

6.

The I.P.K.F burned the sixty dead bodies
on the hospital rubbish heap three days later.
There were no post mortems. Twelve
had decomposed to such an extent,
the names they had once carried
turned to ash in the communal pyre.

7.

After, we walked a tightrope between life and death.
When they brought in injured I.P.K.F
for us to treat, we had to swallow our feelings.
The moment they entered the gates
they turned from aggressor to patient.
Our duty was clear.

8.

Every year, families, survivors, staff and patients
gather to commemorate the dead, whose photos
plaque the wall near the entrance to the hospital.
Men and women, ageing each year, garland faces
wearing 80s haircuts and moustaches.
We are practiced at commemorating our dead.
This is what we are good at.

9.

On the 26th anniversary of the killings
the Indian Government donated scanners
to the X-Ray Block, and requested
that staff remove the memorial
placed at the entrance to the hospital.

On the 26th anniversary of the killings
the survivors, staff and patients
lit the flame of remembrance as usual
and held fast the names of their dead.

10.

Tamil Guardian 22 October 2023. Photo. Image description, embellished.

A group of people have gathered in front of a glass fronted notice board. It is large and institutional, in a non-descript corridor painted cream. Twists of fairy lights and flower garlands are draped across it. A table spread with a white cloth has been placed in front of it, and bordering the edge, are 21 little deepam lamps. Some have been lit. Behind them, a kuthuvillaku and a white pillar candle.

The candlelight flickers on the face of a little girl reaching for a handful of jasmine from a woman. She will place them alongside the mound of blossoms already laid on the table. There are other children lining up to do the same. There are only two old people present. 36 years after the massacre there are no other mothers or fathers left to recite the names of the dead.

11.

Of the ordinary people who were murdered
whether patients or visiting their loved ones,
several were burnt unidentified.
Of those whose names survived
there were
    4 school children. 2 drivers. 2 business managers. 7 mothers.
    4 labourers. 1 carpenter. 1 co-operative society worker. 1 baby.
    2 salesmen. 1 postal worker. 1 cook. 4 old people. 1 harbour
    worker.
    1 security guard. 1 banker. 1 technological assistant.
    background unknown, men 3. background unknown, women 4.

The Naming of Names 3

Jamunakumari	Janagaraja	Jeevamalar	Jeevanathan
Jegarajasingam	Jegatheesan	Jeyalingham	Jeyamalina
Jeyamathy	Jeyanathan	Jeyanthi	Jeyapalan
Jeyaraj	Jeyaram	Jeyaratnam	Jogeswary
Jothyvadivel	Kailaikkutti	Kajan	Kajenthini
Kala	Kalaichselvan	Kalanithy	Kamala
Kamalarasan	Kamini	Kanagalingam	Kanagamalar
Kanagasabai	Kanageswary	Kanakaiya	Kananathan
Kandarasa	Kandasamy	Kannakai	Kannan
Kanoji	Kanthaiya	Kanthalingam	Kanthamuthu
Kanthaperumal	Kanthapodi	Kanthasamy	Kanthasivam
Kanthavanam	Kantheepan	Kapilan	Karikaran
Karmilara	Karthigesu	Karthika	Karunairasa
Karunanithy	Karunaratnam	Karupalagu	Karuppaiah
Karuvalthamby	Kasinathar	Kasipathiyar	Kasun
Kasupathy	Kathambanathan	Kathar	Kathiramali
Kathirgamanathan	Kathirkamar	Kaththan	Katpagam
Keerthika	Kenkatharan	Kethatam	Kiddinapillai
Kidnan	Kili	Kilisras	Kiliyan
Kiritharan	Kirubai	Kirubakaran	Kirubananthy
Kirubaratnam	Kisnasamy	Kobalasinkam	Kodalingam
Kokuleswary	Konamalai	Kopickannan	Kopigan
Kowshiga	Krishanthi	Krishnakumar	Krishnamoorthy
Kubenthiran	Kuddipavun	Kuganantharasa	Kugathas
Kugasaravanamalai	Kulanthai	Kulanthaivadivel	Kulasingam
Kumar	Kumarasamy	Kumuthini	Kunabalasingam
Kunamani	Kunarasa	Kunaratnam	Kunaseelan
Kunasegaram	Kunasingam	Kuppan	Kurnamma
Kurukulam	Kurunathan	Kurus	Kurusamy
Kusalakumari	Latheep	Lavan	Laxmanan

These Were Their Names

What does it feel like to sound
these half-used names of half-lived lives?
Aru-lam-pa-lam, a golden blessing.
Arul-muga-nathan, a man with a wondrous face.
Aru-na-cha-lam, a hill of intense fire.

Asokan was to live a life without sorrow.
Bavani was to be a giver of life.
Geetha carried the music of the Gods in her hair.
And so did Ragini. Jasotha was a gift from God.
Kavitha, a poem.

Piriyalini was a woman in love.
Nesathurai, a man filled with love.
Seenithambi was a little boy made of sugar.
Seevaratnam, a child of light.
So many names bound by a thousand soft blessings.
So many names turned to dust and ash.

Balasuntharam was a beautiful child.
Tharshini, a beautiful offering.
Thiyagarajan was one who sacrificed himself for others.
Yogenthiran was the one who chose to serve.
And Chelliah, Kumutha, Kunchithambi (darling boy),
Manokaran, Rasamohan, Thilagesvari
were the names of the beloved, the cherished ones,
the burning invocations of life.

In Memory II
for Chutty

Her father scooped her up,

stroked a grit-lined eye
and slackened lips

and breathed a lonely aiyo.

As she had done
a few days before.

Until stilled by two gunshots
until held under water

until gathered by the sea
she flowed to the seashore

where she now lies
wearing her corals and pearls.

புதைகுழிப் பாடல்

by Cheran

அவன் தனியே
அவர்களோ மூவர்
முகம் தெரியா இருள்
அவர்களுடைய மனதைப் போல

தன்னுடைய புதைகுழியைத்
தானே வெட்டும் அவலம்
நேர்ந்தபோது
அவன் என்ன உணர்ந்திருப்பான்
என்பது
வார்த்தைக்குள் அகப்படாத
குரூரம்.

அந்தப் புதைகுழியின் மேல்
காற்றில்
உறைந்து போயிருக்கின்றன
அவன் இறுதியாகச்
சொன்ன வார்த்தைகள்

காற்று அவற்றைக்
கொண்டு செல்லாது
மழையும் சூரியனும்
கிட்டவும் நெருங்கா

அவன் சொல்லாத வார்த்தைகளோ
மண்ணுட் போய்
மண்ணிலிருந்து மரத்துட் போய்
அங்கிருந்து கிளைக்கு
கிளையில் இருந்து இலைக்கு
இலையிலிருந்து காற்றில்

இடையறாமல்
அலையலையாக எழுந்துகொண்டிருக்கிறது.

அந்தப் புதைகுழியின் மேல்
பிசாசு இல்லை
தெய்வமும் இல்லை
நினைவுச் சின்னம் எனவும் ஒன்றில்லை

ஆளரவமற்ற இரவுத் தெருவின்
ஒற்றை விளக்குப் போல
உதிரியாய் ஒரு பட்டிப் பூ
அதன் மீது
காலம் தன்னுடைய கொடூர
நகங்களைப் பதித்துள்ளது.

அவனுடை இறுதி வார்த்தைகளில்
இருந்தது
நமது தேசத்தின் உயிர்.

Grave Song
by Cheran, a translation

Alone with the three whose faces
and hearts were hidden in darkness

he dug his own grave.

His distress, the horrors he felt,
were trapped within his final words

which congealed in the air
above that grave.

The wind would not permit the rain
nor the sun to approach them.

Those unspoken words sank
into the soil entering the roots

of trees. The unceasing wind
drew them upwards in waves

radiating them along branches
from leaf to leaf and beyond.

There are no ghosts above that grave.
Nor gods.
There is no memorial stone.

Encased in the cruel grip of time,
a single patti flower grows

upon his grave, burning bright
like a solitary lamp on a darkened street.

In his final words lives
the life of our land.

Sonyeosang (Statue of Peace)
A Response to Cheran's 'Grave Song'

She sits in a square in Seoul, wordless,
hands clenched, staring steadfastly
at the Japanese embassy.

She is whom the Japanese had called
female ammunition,
units of war supplies, public toilets.

Immovable in snow, wind or sun
she cradles a thousand wounds
a thousand tears, a thousand scars.

Her voice, an unending reproach,
is carried by the wind past street corners,
paddy fields and pine forests.

A bird on her shoulder
connects those who gaze on her
to those who have escaped to the sky.

While behind her gaze, the shadows
of those who have grown old invisible,
lengthen in the sun.

The Naming of Names 4

We lay their names, as we have laid their lives, at the feet of God
the Father, the Son and the Holy Ghost.

Alponsparula	Ansalathevy	Antanit	Anthonippillaiparnanthu
Anthonymuttu	Anthonythas	Battic	Bayars
Chrisrinamma	Deluxan	Deluxi	Dias
Devin	Devit	Donald	Donas
Donposko	Dorasdyuk	Edman	Edvert
Edvin	Eliaz	Eliseamma	Fernando
Florence	Francis	Herbert	Imelda
Inmanuvellembet	Iruthayanathan	Iyakkopillai	Janetqueen
Jenitta	Jenovi	Jerat	Jesunayakam
Jesuthas	Jesuthasan	Jeyagoban	Jeyakobal
Jeyathasan	John	Johnbaptist	Johnson
Jonas	Joseph	Josephine	JosephJud
Josephs	Jovan	Judmohanathas	Kamalitta
Kamalthasan	Kanistan	Kapiriyelpillai	Kaspar
Kemalatha	Kinsly	KiresPretti	Kiresu
Kirusdi	Kirusnanantham	Kolinlemport	Komanathas
Kondusiyas	Konsala	Konsedda	Krishdiyan
Kurusumuthu	Kurusupillai	Kurusuthasan	Lambert
Loosiya	Marimuthu	Mariyamanikam	Mariyamma

Mariyanayakam	Mariyampillai	Mariyamuthu	Mariyan
Mariyanayagam	Mariyarajith	Mariyathas	Mariyelpillai
Markupillai	Martin	Mary	Maryamma
Melrose	Menis	Merikarmilarani	Mesiyas
Michael	Miyes	Mosan	Nikkilas
Nelsan	Nikkalasjud	Niksan	Parnanthu
Peliseeyan	Penadict	Peter	Peterpol
Philip	Philippaiya	Philippupillai	Ponibas
Poulinrasa	Preeton	Prinkgespek	Pulorans
Regina	Rerans	Robert	Robinson
Roche	Romikaran	Romila	Samuel
Sangunin	Sebamalaimuthu	Sebamani	Sebasthiyampillai
Sebestian	Senjude	Seronconsenter	Seviyar
Simon	Solomon	Soosaiappu	Soosaipillai
Stalin	Stanic	Stanly	Susainathan
Susainathankuru	Sylvestar	Tharsiyas	Thaveethu
Thomas	Thombaimiyes	Vathsalamary	Velicia
Victor	Vincent	Wenceslaus	Xavier
Yuliyas	Yute	Yutechristin	

Two Islands

'Nine Civilians Killed in Naval Attack'
The Island 4 January 1993
filed by Reuters in Colombo.

'Navy Demolishes Tiger Boats'
The Island 5 January 1993
reported by Shamindra
Fernando

On Saturday night a flotilla of boats
crossing Jaffna lagoon, were fired on
by navy patrol boats, because to cross
the Jaffna lagoon is prohibited by the Navy.

Blasting Four Fibre Glass Dinghies'
Killing Over a Dozen Persons'
Joint Operations Command revealed.

Sixteen civilian boats carrying
twenty people each. Trying to escape
to the safety of the other shore.

'The dinghies operated by the Sea Tigers
were moving in convoy, when swooped
on by Navy patrol boats.'

People panicked, screamed, shouted.
Women, children, killed by gunfire.

Navy patrol craft confronted the boats
and were successful in controlling
Sea Tiger activities in the Jaffna lagoon.

Only six of the flotilla reached safety.

'All boats trying to break the government
ban will be dealt with'.

*Many of the bodies recovered were badly mutilated. Tharmaraja, the
deceased Director of Education had an eye gouged out. His thigh too had
a deep cut. The corpse of a lady which reached the shore was without its
head. Of the five or so boats towed away, the bodies of the dead were placed
in one boat and the boat was set on fire. Many of the dead also had gaping
wounds suggesting that these were caused by cannon rather than small arms.
University Teachers for Human Rights Report no. 10. 15th January 1993.*

How to Dispose of Tamils

1. Build a huge bonfire.

2. Dig a huge pit.

3. Acid decimates the features of the dead.
    Disrupts identification.

4. Paddy husks make good tinder.
    Paddy fields good cremation grounds.

5. When clearing villages
    pile the bodies inside houses.
    Set them on fire.
    Ash contains no names.

6. You can burn them in forests
    you can burn them in fields
    place them in tyres
    and burn them in the streets.

7. Keep a plentiful supply of kerosene
    and tar for use in such manoeuvres.

8. Throw bodies out of helicopters over jungles.

9. Give them spades.
    Make them dig their own graves.

10. Make them lie down on the road.
    Drive tanks over them.

11. Babies are easily dispatched
    under hobnailed boots.
    Or by slicing open a pregnant belly.

12. Parade able-bodied Tamil men
    through a Sinhala village.
    Announce that they are L.T.T.E cadres.
    When you shoot them
    your witnesses will swear
    to the death of combatants.

13. Chop off their heads
    and dump them into the sea.
    No face, no name, no crime.

14. Also, chop off their hands.

15. Cluster bombs and Claymore mines
    make your job much easier.

16. Wells are usefully located
    in each garden. Also, usefully deep.

17. Septic tanks too make useful
    disposal places.

18. Use Sinhala prisoners.
    Offer them an amnesty.
    Offer them pay-per-corpse.

19. Remove clothing before disposing bodies.
    Too many skeletons are identified by them.

20. Use Emergency Resolution powers
    to prevent post-mortems.
    No identification, no accusation.
    No name, no crime.

Some of the methods used by the military when disposing of bodies in Sri Lanka.

The Naming of Names 5

Lingeswaran	Logeswary	Logitharaja	Lubashini
Madusan	Mageswary	Mahadeva	Mahalingam
Mahaluxsumy	Mahendramoorthy	Mainthini	Malai
Malarvili	Malligathevi	Manavel	Mangalanayaki
Manikam	Manivel	Maniyam	Manjulathevi
Mannivannan	Manoranjitham	Manothiga	Marisaleen
Markandu	Mathavan	Mathukaran	Mayiluppoodi
Meena	Menon	Menperis	Methini
Mithila	Mithura	Mohamed	Mohan
Mohanasundari	Moothathamby	Mukamadrasik	Muniyandi
Munusamy	Murugaiah	Murugan200than	Murugasapillai
Murugesan	Murugathas	Muthaiah	Muthukumar
Muthulingam	Mylvaganam	Nachipillai	Nadesam
Nagadas	Nagaiah	Nagaloosini	Nagamani
Nagathesi	Nagendraraja	Nageswari	Nahuleswari
Najimutheen	Nallaiyah	Nallamma	Nallamuthu
Namanathan	Namasivayam	Nannithambi	Nantheswaran
Narayanasingham	Nareskumar	Narumalathevy	Nathan
Natkunam	Navamani	Navaratnam	Navaz
Neelamegam	Neelavathy	Neminathan	Neru
Nesamma	Nigethanan	Nilayinar	Nimali
Nirmaladevi	Nirmaleswaran	Nisantharuban	Nishanthan
Nitharshini	Noyalimmanu	Packiyam	Paddaiyamma
Pakeerathan	Pakianathan	Palagapoody	Palakumar
Palan	Palani	Palaniyandi	Palapaskaran
Palaratnam	Palaththai	Palayogini	Palenthiran
Palipoodi	Panchalingam	Pandiyan	Pannichelvam
Panugopal	Paralokanathan	Paramalingam	Paramanantham
Paramasamy	Paramasingham	Parameswaran	Paranchsoothy
Parashakthy	Parasuraman	Parathy	Parimalam

II

The Naming of Names 6

My father's name was Prince Selvadurai Selvachandran. His
father was Samuel Saravanamuttu Selvadurai. Tamils do not use
surnames – your name is sufficiently your own. My mother's name
was Brenda Pamela Kay. Her father's name was Krishnaiyar – a
brahmin from India – who anglicised his name when rejected by
his family for marrying a Christian from Ceylon.

I was christened Priscilla Sasikala Selvachandran. In the country
where I was born my Anglicised first name denoted that I was a
Christian. My surname that I was Tamil. My name the marker of
my difference.

Tamil women are known by their own names. A matrilineal
throwback from pre-colonial times. I should be known as T.
Shash. My birth certificate, written in Tamil, on a trilingual
form (Tamil, Sinhala and English) has my mother's pencilled
translations for our asylum application. My name in Tamil,
சசிகலா, should have transferred across to English as 'Sasikala'.
But my mother, clinging to her Brahmin roots, sanskritised me by
using the alien ஷ/ sh. In the U.K I became Shash.

The naming of names and the way we carry them helps us write
the story our children will make their own. By repetition on
certificates, censuses and passports, they seem set in stone. And
yet, through war, necessity or custom my family's use of names has
been water-like, flowing through languages and prejudices. An
unforeseen consequence of all our unmoorings.

The Intimacy of Scorpions

These are the things I miss:
Squat mango trees.
Benny's old Ambassador carrying
fourteen to school each day.
The earth-smell on the first day of the rains.
The warmth of rain.
The intimacy of scorpions.
The surprise suddenness of nightfall.
Iddiyapam and mutton rolls.
The crack, then thud, of falling coconuts.
Parrots in neem trees.
The hiss of a tarantula on fire.

காணாது போன சிறுவர்கள்

by Illavallai Wijayenthiran

ஆலமரமிருக்கும்
கீழோ, ஊஞ்சல்
ஆடிக் களிக்கவென
நீள விழுதிருக்கும்.

சற்று அப்பால்
பொன்னொச்சி பூத்துச்
சிரித்திருக்கும்.
கிழக்காய்,
மாரி மழை நடுவில்
ஊற்றெடுத்துப் பரந்துபடும்
குளமிருக்கும்.

கட்டைப் பனைமரத்தைக்
கப்பலாக்கிக்
கால்த்துடுப்பில் நீர்கடக்கும்
சிறுவர்களை மட்டும்
காணேன்.

பலகாலம் குண்டெறிந்தும்
தலைகுனியாப்
பனைமரத்தின் மீதேறிப்
'பால்' கறக்கும்
முதியவரைக் கேட்டேன்.

"காசுவயல்க் கதிரறுக்கக்
கனடா போய்ச்
சேர்ந்தார்கள்"
என்றார் கவலையுடன்.

The Missing Children
by Illavallai Wijayenthiran, a translation

The hanging roots of the banyan tree,
like swinging ropes, promise hours of fun.
Around it, the ponnochchi flowers
laugh in the breeze. To the East,
a pond overflows in the rainy season.
By its shore a boat made of dead palm wood
on which to voyage repeatedly.
The only thing missing from this scene
were the children.

        I asked an old man
climbing coconut trees, their heads
still unbent despite the bombings,
where the children were. They have gone
to harvest the money fields of Canada
he replied, with sadness.

Here Be Dragons
A response to Wijayendran's 'The Missing Children'

You are not of this world, my voyager.
Your head never still on your pillow
you fly on the upbeat of a murmuration
look down on the vastness below
and draw songlines – connections, parallels –
which make sense only to you. A cartographer,
a tousle headed dreamer, fighting giants
by day, riding with the Valkyrie at night.
What do you think of those who don't have your gift
to see the improbable in the ordinary?
My son –
may your flights of fantasy lead you to lands
where the warmth of the sun will welcome you.
And may the East Wind always bear you back home.

Three Friends Set Out One Day

the one going South arrived first,
having crossed imaginary borders
made real by checkpoints and gun turrets.

The one who went East got lost
in a forest where she was rescued
by an ambush of passing tigers.

Not long after, she was photographed
by trophy hunters, having died
making their wishes come true.

The one who journeyed West didn't arrive
until the days turned into months
and months into seasons.

In a land of snow and ice, her face
grew dark, losing the light she had borrowed
from the moon back home.

The Dubs Amendment 25 April 2016

Bellingham Clifton-Brown Carmichael Duncan-Smith Wilson Wragg Holobone Malthouse Duddridge Fernandes Allan Baker Stevenson Costa Watkinson Lefroy Green Morris Cleverly Donelan Dowden Elwood Graham Gyimah Parish Scully Selous Tracey Heaton-Jones Kawczynski Norman Carswell Baldwin Barwell Borwick Cartlidge Knight Jenrick Lumley Thomas Tolhurst Warman Jenkin Stewart Hammond Argar Miller Ghani Williamson Howell Leslie Djanogly Morris Gillan Beresford Nokes Rutley Mackintosh Huddleston Stephenson McPartland Elphicke Grant Dunne Grieve Harper Dining Ansell Churchill Davies Mills Coffey Jones Clarke Burrowes

McCartney	Shannon Cash	Spelman
Drax Burt	Ellis Field Freer	Leadsom Robinson
Gale Gibb Glen	Gove Patel Prisk	Metcalfe Solloway Murrison
Quin Raab Rudd	Tyrie Hart	Whittaker Loughton Pritchard
Hunt Hurd Lord	Main Mann	Holloway Pursglove
Blunt Berry Bingham	Tugendhat Fox	Merman Sandbach
Lee Mak Bone Bebb	Berry Smith	Spencer Robertson
White Offord Nuttall	Murray Pawsey	Whately Wollaston
Barclay Penning Newton	Johnson	Menzies Opperman
Mordant Kinahan Williams	Lopresti	Swayne Skidmore
Paterson Rosindell Heaton-	Harris Wood	Milling Redwood
Jayawardena Sunak	Johnson Letwin	Morgan Timpson
Trevelyan Syms Wheeler	Pickles Walker	Herbert Jackson Vickers
Morton Shapps	Fallon Soubry Villiers	Streeter Walker Johnson
Stuart Stride	Evans Evans Smith	Turner Stewart Wiggin
Smith Hall May	Burns Chalk Swire	Poulter Lewis Jenkyns Brazier
Amess Lilley	Fabricant Lewis	Bottomley Hands
Prentis Wright	Lidington Liddell-	Tomlinson McLoughlin
Grainger Clark	Pow Rees-Mogg	Grayling Crabb Lancaster
Whittingdale	Philip Soames	Mowat Gummer Vaizey
Penrose Sturdy	Stewart	Tredinnick Javid

Evennett Freeman Griffiths Goodwill Hancock Bradley Afriyie Aldous Benyon Andrew
Chishti Harrington Haselhurst Henderson Sharma Knight Brokenshire Doyle-Price
Drummond Mackinlay Adams Green Bacon Hinds Pincher Vara Heald Kirby Brady
Frazer Gauke Atkins Baron Halfon Burns Fallon Elliott Campbell Heaped Davies
Foster Hopkins Caulfield Davies Maynard Throup Collins Colvile Double Ellison
Garner Sherbrooke Buckland Latham Jones Charting Leigh Garnier Kennedy Jones
Bruce Howlett Morris Chope Harris Milton Simpson Tomlinson Davies Howarth

they said

as
mobilised
children endure
alone on Europe's
dung heaps. They have
hung up their toys their
drums and their harps. They
have nothing left to sing
in this new land.

Meanwhile faith, hope and charity
lie chained and debased
on Albion's shore.

Illegal Migration Bill

House of Commons, Session 2022-23
30 March 2023

I

A bill to make provision for ▮▮▮▮▮▮▮▮▮▮ *the removal*
from the United Kingdom of ▮▮▮▮▮▮▮▮▮▮▮
▮▮▮▮▮▮▮▮▮▮▮▮▮▮▮▮▮▮▮▮

▮▮▮▮▮▮▮▮▮▮▮▮▮▮ *unaccompanied*
children, ▮▮▮▮▮▮▮ *victims of slavery or human*
trafficking; to make provision ▮▮▮▮▮▮
▮▮▮▮▮▮▮▮ *about* ▮▮▮▮▮
▮▮▮▮▮▮ *the inadmissibility of certain protection and*
▮▮▮ *human rights* ▮▮▮▮▮▮▮▮▮
▮▮▮▮▮▮ *of persons entering the*
United Kingdom. ▮▮▮▮▮▮▮▮
▮▮▮▮

II

A bill to ▮▮▮▮▮▮▮▮▮▮▮▮
▮▮▮▮▮▮▮▮▮▮▮▮▮▮
▮▮▮▮▮▮ *make provision* ▮▮▮▮
▮▮▮▮▮▮▮▮▮▮▮▮▮▮
▮▮▮▮▮▮▮▮▮▮▮▮▮▮
▮▮▮▮▮▮▮▮▮▮▮▮▮▮
▮▮▮ *about the inadmissibility of* ▮▮▮▮▮
▮▮▮▮▮▮▮▮▮▮▮▮▮▮
▮▮▮▮▮▮▮▮▮▮
▮▮▮ *safe and legal routes* ▮▮▮▮
▮▮▮

III

A bill to make provision for ███████████████████████

██

██████████████████████████████ *detention*

██

██

██

██

███

██

███

███

███████

Now in the Sahara

Poor Ritchie went to Africa, and died, as Lamb foresaw, in 1819.
Keats died in 1821, at Rome. C. Lamb is gone, joking to the last.
Monkhouse is dead, and Wordsworth and I are the only two now
living (1841) of that glorious party.
    – Benjamin Haydon Autobiography (London, 1853)

Endymion now lies in the Sahara.
Returned to the mountains of the moon
as a favour to Keats.

Flung into the hot desert sands
by Joseph Ritchie, when dressed
as a Berber nomad he left Tripoli
in search of the kingdom of Timbuktu.
A white man stained brown.

One among five hundred pounds of books,
six hundred pounds of lead for trade,
two camel loads of brown paper
for the preserving of plants, two chests
of arsenic for the killing of insects.

And carried 'over those African sands
immeasurable', *Endymion* now
lies in the Sahara, returned
to the mountains of the moon
as a favour to Keats.

In 1819, just before Joseph Ritchie left on his doomed expedition in search of
Timbuktu, he met Keats at a gathering at Benjamin Haydon's house, and Keats
requested that Ritchie fling a copy of *Endymion* into the Sahara as a favour to him.
A few months later Keats received a letter from Ritchie stating that *Endymion* had
been carried 'o'er those African sands immeasurable'.

The Armada Children's Library

That was the day I returned from school
to find my bookshelves empty. All copies
of my precious *Ambulimama*
had disappeared. Pages filled with kings
and their courts, the wisdom of swamis,
of naughty devas chasing apsaras
around celestial forests. Illustrations
inviting me to take flight on Sarasvati's
swan, or float down from the Himalayas
on Parvati's lotus. All gone.

And in their place a pile of books in English.
Enid Blyton's *Eight O'Clock Tales*,
the Secret Seven, *Mr. Meddle's Muddles*.
Strangers in a feringi lexicon.
A galleon in full sail on their spines.

New words, new clothes

I discarded the words first.

And then, for a while, mute silence.
I watched and learnt like a mynah bird.

அ became A
ஈ became E
இ I changed to a short, sharp I.

After a while through whispers and croaks
new words emerged
in the borrowed tongue of a borrowed land.

Tentative, tiny and uncomplicated
brand new, pain-free little words.
Their strange scrolls flowed around me.

F was once a little Fish
Z was once a piece of Zinc
X was once a great king Xerxes

For the first time I formed an F, wrote
a Z, sounded an X. In the borrowed tongue
of a borrowed land I dressed myself in them.

I abandoned two millennia
of poetry, mythology and history.
No Pallavan or Cholan could claim sovereignty
over my mouth, my tongue, my mind.

In the borrowed tongue of a borrowed land
in single, stuttering, borrowed syllables
I began to talk again

and the new words began to flow.

Crossing the Waters

My mother made me the keeper
of her stories. Of love and loss
and a family in the making.

Of how her grandmother had jumped
from a moving train from Colombo
to Jaffna, to return to the man
she was determined to marry.

Of how in time, her daughter –
my grandmother – chose a man
from across the waters, who unknotted
his Poonul to marry her, a Christian.

Of how when my mother left India
to join my father waiting at the altar,
among her goodbyes was one
that was to be final.

The news of her father's death –
the man she measured all men against –
reached my father by telephone
while she waited to cross the waters.

And he kept it from her.

A silence which wreathed his wedding vows,
curling around the jasmine in her bouquet
and in her hair. It was 1964.
The Ceylonese government

was in a frenzy, expelling
Indian Tamils from the Island.
A second visa would prove impossible
my father judged and sealed his lips tight.

From such beginnings marriages are made.

Poonul: The sacred thread worn by Brahmin boys and men.

III

Blue Lotus Flowers

I

What She Says

Why do you ask me
when he will come?

> He is like the man from the tall hills
> his face hidden by rainclouds.
> The blue of his sapphires glint only
> in the darkness.
> And he comes and goes at will
> like a waterfall crashing down the mountainside.

My tears fall like petals
and wet the plains at his feet.

II

What She Says

I look to the blue hills
and wait for his return.

> His beauty, like the blooms
> of the tiger claw tree,
> is bright and scarlet in the darkness.
> He is gone, like a heron once fed
> flies to another sky.

My tears run like waves
on a salty shore.

III

What She Says

As the morning dew
wets the green plains
he came to me.

        As beautiful as a peacock on the hillside.
        As strong as a bull elephant
        swaying among the young grass.
        Bright as the green parrot
        skimming the mango tree
        he called to me.

My honey rose and flowed.
The bees made soft music
as he drank his fill.

IV

What She Says

In the forest where the sparrow hen
pecks at the Cassia roots
he watched like a stag
warned of a stranger's approach.

                    He was strong and wide like a river.
                    The plowman harvested by his shore
                    and Inthiran rained flowers
                    strewing the ground like a bridal bower.

That was then.
Now I wait for him
trembling for his touch
and my tears water the laurel tree.

V

What She Says

The sun has parched my tears
my bangles slip from my wrist.
Their shards cut my feet
dotting the floor
like the dried kungumum
on my brow line.

> For he has gone to the wasteland
> like a lone hen-eagle searching
> from the branches of the portia tree.
> The mid-day sun burns his feet
> as he stalks, a petulant tiger
> denied its kill.

And here, by my waterless well
bandits threaten my laurel tree.
I have nothing to offer them.
A lizard skittles over the cactus
of my heart.

VI

What She Says

Here by the side of the royal pool
I wait, but he does not come.
He is like the man from the cold shore
scuttling like a crab
to another's bower.

> The cool waters invite me.
> There are no herons
> feeding at my feet.
> The bull elephant has defiled
> the watering hole.

The blue lotus flower opens
its starry petals
and offers a pillow for my head.
The waters rise
washing the salt from my eyes.

This poem has been written in the style of early classical Tamil poetry as laid out in the *Tolkaappiyam*. The poem mirrors the akam poems of the classical Sangam period (second century CE) which deal with the interior landscape of lovers and married life. Akam poems use flora and fauna to describe the moods of the narrator - the interior mirrors the exterior and the reader is able to place the path of a relationship based on the landscapes the poems invoke.

Patyegarang

She clutched her collection of words
bulbous, tightly packed, ageless
like the flame heads of the waratah
burning skywards along the songlines
of the Eoran people.

Bógee – to bath or to swim
Nánga – to sleep, *Patá* – to eat,
naa – to see, *Nyínadyımíŋa* –
You stand between me and the fire.

In Dreamtime the waratah bloomed white
until an encounter between a hawk
and a wonga pigeon above it
turned the white flower red.

Red seeds, red words. From her hands to his
passed perfectly formed capsules of time
and memory. A florescence
of a crimson, breathing language.

Dteéwara – hair, *NGára* – to hear.
Catching fish on a hook made from bark.
Putuwá, she said. 'I warm my hand
by the fire and then gently
squeeze your hand in mine'.

When he sailed home he carried with him
her voice compact in his notebooks
and a single waratah head.
Gwàra buráwà – The wind is falling, she said.
Buŋabaoú buk ŋyıniwàgolàŋ
I will make a book for you, he replied.

In 1787 Patyegarang, a young girl from the Eoran tribe, who inhabited the area
which would become Sydney, taught the Eoran language to William Dawes, a
young English botanist and engineer. The Eorans were soon wiped out by smallpox
and European colonialism and the only record of their language survives in the
notebooks Dawes kept of his time with Patyegarang.

I was Na'amah

I was known by many names and now by none.

I was Na'amah, the pleasant one
mother to all creation. The hourglass
gathered pace in my shadow.

I was Emzara, Betenos, Barthenon
wheat and millet swayed to my song.
Around my feet grew common reed
papyrus sedge and bullrushes.

I was Haykel in Arabic.
Through my mouth sun rose flowers, blue pimpernel
and yachnuk spoke a language of their own.
Cumin and chamomile formed my veil.

In Georgian I was T'ajar, a temple.
Bitter herbs formed my seat.
Out of my left arm grew olive trees,
cypress and cedar of Lebanon. Red bush,
date palms and myrrh out of my right.

I was Nemzar in Armenian.
I knew every lacewing of every petal
every wrinkled bark, each sharp thorn.
I twirled every leaf in dewdrops
and hid a covenant into each rotund kernel.

I was Emzara, Noyemza. Norea to the Gnostics.
The Babylonians called me Tytea.
I was the sunrise of creation
the moon glow of eternity.
In the *Book of Jasher* I was Na'amah
the pleasant one.
Now I am known only as the wife of Noah.

Becky in the Garden, Dancing with Butterflies

The purple buddleia bows its head
garlanding her hair, laden with hundreds
and thousands of butterflies she says,
dancing in the long green grass.

In and among the trees and stumps
like a cloud of paper kisses they rise,
mimicking her movements
chasing sunshine on dry crisp wings.

When she is still for a moment –
a jaguar stalking her prey
or just lost in the wonder of being –
they reach for the purple spears again.

A stillness which does not last. For she is all
movement and light, catching their iridescence,
in the wideness of her smile, their stained glass
colours in the shine of her eyes.

Such lives will fit while the buddleia blooms
until time propels in new tomorrows.
But today, the paper partners flit in the sunlight
and Becky is in the garden, dancing

with butterflies. Her wings yet unfolded,
unaware that she will one day fly.

Jane Eyre looks on 'The Death of General Wolfe'

She had arrived too early, or they were late –
was ushered into a back parlour,
a welcoming fire after sixteen hours
teeth shattering in a rattlebox.
Wilting, she waits at this last post
with George III, the Prince of Wales
and General Wolfe.

Jane Eyre looks on the death of General Wolfe:
red clashing with blue and buff,
a stormy sky, a tattered flag, a tableau
in disarray. The Mohawk warrior crouching
in the foreground, muscles clenched,
coiled in naked curiosity. Tattooed and feathered,
his rich ochre leeches the seeping claret
of the dying General, his master.
Grey eyes probe his shuttered distant gaze,
a painted fellow to that natural force
pacing in bondage the battlements
of Thornfield. The scene has been set.

Troubled, uneasy, she drops her gaze,
turns to the hearth and waits.
At Thornfield, the aroused captive
explodes from his crenelated prison.
Piloting his future, man, horse and dog
thunder irrepressibly towards
the George Inn at Millcote.

Jane Eyre Chapter 11; Benjamin West's painting 'The Death of General Wolfe' 1770

Ann Lowe 1953

'A coloured woman made it.'

No name, no significance.

Cotton, bobbin
spin the wheel.

The cotton flower blooms
in the postbellum South.

Pick, pick, unstitch

Fifty yards of ivory silk
tucked and banded

like her great-grandmother
flicking the bolls.

Quick eyes, precise fingers.

The cotton flower blooms
in an endless summer.

Bridal white for a Senator's wife.

Back stitch, chain stitch
blind whip stitch

cotton reel, satin finish.

'Who made your dress Miss Bouvier?'
'A coloured woman made it.'

No name, no voice.

The cotton flower blooms
a lineage of seamstresses.

Pin, tuck
a portrait neckline

full, full skirt
embroidered flowers

cotton flowers

circles tracing patterns
concentric, widening

like her great-grandmother's
arms stroking the cotton crop.

The cotton flower blooms
in manacled abundance.

Watered silk, french knot
couching blanket stitch

bridal white for a President's wife.

'Who made your dress Miss Bouvier?'
'A coloured woman made it.'

Vera, Waiting

She had prepared for a telegram
prepared for what she would say
to the Post Office boy. Prepared
her retreat to her room, to slit open
the envelope and allow the news
to make a sortie into her mind.
An assault anticipated.
Yet when the news came, it was by telephone.
And she was in Brighton, not Buxton –
her dug-out two hundred miles away –
her parapet bare of barbed wire.
And as the mud of Louvencourt
silted over his body, her life zig-zagged
out of control and she realised
that what she had thought possible
was now a sap abandoned in no-man's land.
A collapsed line soon to be overrun
in a soil which would always smell
of sweat and blood, and of violets
dying in Ploegsteert Wood.

IV

When David Heard

after Thomas Tomkins

> When David heard
> that Absalon was dead, he went
> up to his chamber and wept.

It begins quietly. The trebles leading,
the altos and then the tenors joining.
It is sorrow. Wave after wave
borne on a wall of homophonic sound.
The contrapuntal boom of the basses,
a thud from the heart of a father.

'Oh my son, my son, my son.' Repeated
over twenty-five bars. A mind unable
to move beyond the keening of his name.
'Absalon, my son' plucked from the stave
by voices harmonised in lament and regret.

'Would God I had died for thee.'
The interval from the 'would' to 'God'
begins as a rising minor 3rd, and retreats,
almost immediately, to a rising semitone.
The startling immediacy of despair.

The tessitura rises, the rhythm is charged
as this private grief moves from the bedchamber
to flow around the quire in song.
Then the music ebbs, surprises
the listener, shifts from the minor

to coalesce around the major tonic.
The other side of pain.
Pleasing to the ear, but maybe,
not to the mind. Would God
all grief run a course like this.

The Naming of Names 7

She wore her age like a shroud of light and ash.
From deep within her came a chanting:
Balachandran, Chandrakumar, Chandramohan
Nilajini, Santhiya, Jeyamohan.
Names which held the silver of moonlight.
Kalanithy, Kalickuddy, Kalimuthu, Kaliraja,
Chandrasekeran – one whose hair is adorned by the moon
Gnanachandran – one filled with the wisdom of the moon.

He wore his age on a face shrouded by sound.
From him came the knell of bells:
Aaron, Abraham, Aquinas, Anton,
Alexshanthar, Alfonse, Alistan, Alfred,
Alvin, Anchsala, Anthony, Albert.
Christuraja, Cyrilappar, Cruz, David...

Do you hear us? From the whites of his eyes
came a whisper which filled the air with music.
The old woman's blood sang in answer.
We are the keepers of dead names.
Soul bearers looking for faces to open.
The heirs of Achuthan – the boy who will never die.

Anantham, Alagan, Ananthapuvanan –
a joyful sky filled with flowers.
Ariyamalar – oh flower of knowledge
Ariyanayakam – oh heroic knowledge
Ariyaratnam – the jewel of knowledge
Hear our prayers of penance.
Hear our prayers of remembrance.

Muthumai Kolam

Feet planted in perfect balance
she bends each morning deftly
dotting the floor. Each pulli a prayer
each sikku a curving embrace.

The fish, birds and flowers, her suns
moons and stars, her patterned privations
flow through from the outside in,
a propitiation –

so that he might not disappear
into the darkness, so that her lips
might call him forth from the unknown.
Each curve and syllable of his name
a proclamation of his absence.

For months she has performed
these muthumai kolams for him.

While somewhere
he washes her feet daily
with his tears.

Muthumai Kolam in Tamil means 'patterns of old age'. Kolams are the patterns
drawn by Tamil women in front of houses as an offering to deities. They are made up
of dots (pulli) and strokes (sikku). This poem is about the Tamil 'disappeared' in Sri
Lanka.

The Last Mango Tree

The last mango tree stands alone
in a garden that was once full
of other mango trees and coconut
palms. It holds out its arms, golden
with fruit, and looks at the rusted, shut gate.
Grass grows beneath and around it
and the birds have grown accustomed
to its solitude. The last mango tree
waits, remembering those years when children
clung to its branches, women picked its fruit –
green for pickling, honeyed orange for eating.
The last mango tree knows that its branches
hold the secrets of a lost people.
It stands guarding memories, surrounded
by abandoned and derelict life.

The Naming of Names 8

Parimelalagar	Parthima	Parvati	Paskaralingam
Pastiampillai	Pasumai	Pasupathi	Pathmanathan
Paththinian	Pattgunaraja	Pavalam	Pavalanathan
Pavan	Perambalam	Peries	Perinban
Periyanpillai	Perumal	Pethamparam	Pilenthiran
Pillainayagam	Pirapa	Pirakala	Pirasanna
Pirathees	Piyanthan	Polenthirarasa	Pologanathan
Ponnampalam	Ponnuththurai	Poomani	Poopathy
Pooranam	Prasath	Pratheepa	Premalatha
Premasasikala	Premathas	Printhini	Priyatharsini
Pukenthiran	Pulendran	Punniyalingam	Pushpakaran
Puspalatha	Puspaleela	Puspavathy	Puvanasekaram
Puvaneswary	Puvi	Radhakrishnana	Radhika
Ragenthiran	Rageswary	Ragunathan	Raguvarnan
Rajadurai	Rajamohan	Rajasundaram	Rajeev
Rajenthiran	Rajeswary	Rajitha	Raju
Ramachchandran	Ramaiya	Ramajeyam	Ramalingam
Ramasamy	Rameshkumar	Rameshwaran	Ranimalar
Ranjan	Ranjanesan	Ranjithkumar	Rasamanickam
Rasaiah	Rasakopal	Rasakumar	Rasalingam
Rasamma	Rasanayagam	Rasathurai	Rasharam
Rashmy	Ratheeswaran	Ratnaraja	Ravichandran
Ravindrakumar	Ravinthiran	Ravishankar	Ravivarman
Raviveeran	Renuka	Rilvan	Rishad
Rishikesan	Rohini	Rubankuruvi	Rukthi
Rukumani	Rupavathani	Ruthiralingam	Sabanathan
Sabapathy	Sabaratnam	Sabeser	Sagathevan
Sagayanayagi	Sajeevan	Sakayanathan	Sakthivel
Salamipillai	Samithamby	Sammanthan	Sangarapillai
Sangeetha	Sankar	Sanmokathasan	Santhakumar

The Naming of Names 9

They blazed on Kathiramalai,
these bright ones, these givers of light.

Ushananthan and Uthayakumar named
after the god of dawn and his son.

Savithri was the daughter of the sun.
and Anushya, the kiss of sunrise.

Sudamani burned bright as lightning.
Chitra and Revathy, two stars on fire.

Sayanthini's hair was braided with twilight.
and Prakash shimmered with radiance.

Gnanaseelan was filled with a divine glow.
Jegatheepan was the light of the world.

And Dilani, the iridescent one, was to shine for ever.

Bitter Waters

See these lines on my up turned palm.

They are the rivers of death
that have washed my land.

Flowing first in trickles,
then streams, then in torrents:

they are the swell of voices
that have cried out our pain.

They lie etched on my skin, coursing
through the creases and ridges

to pool into stories of names.

I shall tell of these,
I shall tell of these,
for generations to come.

See these hands all twisted and bent.

These are the scars I bear
instead of children.

O Motherland, don't look to me
for your warrior.

Nanthikadal Lagoon

The waters of the lagoon were brackish
with the sweat and tears of twenty-six years.
Every eye, every name and story which began
as a caress and ended with a sob
made its way in trickles to the lagoon's shore.
Here the salty lives pooled –
filled the mouths of those who swam in them
with bitterness. Tried to stop their hearts.

Sorrow made a mirror-lake of longing
in which people found themselves. Sorrow
made a peep-hole, offering glimpses
of forgotten laughter. Sorrow chronicled
a bloody end as the sun dripped fire,
emptying itself. Come immortal waters,
Nanthini, plait my hair with your sodden
breast bones and ribcages.

The Sri Lankan civil war reached its bloody end by the banks of this lagoon. The
UN estimates that between 40,000 – 70,000 civilians were killed in the last three
months of the war; the majority from being herded into No Fire Zones, set up by
the Sri Lankan Army, by the banks of Nanthikadal Lagoon.

The Naming of Names 10

Santhanam	Santhirakanthan	Santhiraleela	Santhiya
Sapapathipillai	Sarasu	Sarmila	Sarojadevi
Sarukesan	Sasikala	Sathananthan	Sathasivan
Satheesan	Sathiyarupan	Satkunarasa	Savunthararasa
Seethevipillai	Seetha	Segaran	Sellachi
Sellaiah	Sellam	Sellamuthu	Sellathurai
Selva	Selvakanthini	Selvakumar	Selvanayaki
Selvaratnam	Senthilkumar	Shanmugalingam	Shanmugavadivel
Shantakumari	Shanthy	Shanuka	Sharmila
Sinnaiah	Sinnakutti	Sinthuja	Sithamparapillai
Sithuran	Sittampalam	Sivabalasingam	Sivaguru
Sivamurthy	Sivanathan	Sivanesan	Sivapakkiyam
Sivapatham	Sivaranjini	Sivasothy	Siyamala
Somasuntharam	Sothilingam	Sripaskaran	Subashini
Subramaniam	Sujatha	Sulaiman	Sulaxsana
Sullthan	Sumithra	Sunil	Suntharalingam
Suresh	Susantha	Suseela	Suventhiran
Thalayasingam	Thambaiah	Thambimuttu	Thamenthiny
Thamilselvan	Thamilvanan	Thanabalasingam	Thangamani
Thangaratnam	Thangeswaran	Thanuskody	Thabaseelan
Tharani	Tharmakulasingam	Tharmalingam	Tharmaraja
Tharsana	Thatsuthan	Thavaluxsumy	Thavam
Thaventhiran	Thayalasingam	Theepa	Theivanayagam
Theiventhiran	Thenuga	Thevagi	Thevakumar
Thevananthini	Thevanayaki	Thevasakayam	Thevathasan
Thileepkumar	Thillainadarasa	Thinesh	Thiruchelvam
Thisaiveerasingam	Thuraiappa	Thuraiswamy	Thusyenthiran
Thuthikaran	Thuvani	Thuvaragathevy	Ulaganathan
Umaithamby	Umakanthan	Umarani	Urkanasamy
Urugan	Ushanthini	Uthayasooriyan	Uvarasini

The Sinhala Only Act, 1956

Tamil words that lilt, soothing as a lullaby
on a mother's breath. Their isaioli   *melody*
nourishing our uyir, a life force   *life*
marked on a stave imagined
millennia ago. In whispers
of promises they show themselves
as paadal and kathai and kavithai.   *songs; stories; poetry*
Our generations were formed
by their fluid naatiyam, our voices   *dance*
tuned to their scripted sangeetham.   *hymns*
And when we dreamed, our dreams erupted
in அs and இs and உs: building blocks   *Aaa; Eee; Uuu*
of a nation now without a homeland,
a people now without a place.

And when in '56 they tried to silence
your innisai, gag your uyiroli   *sweet melody; vowels*
and eradicate your meiyelluthal   *consonants*
we took to the streets carrying
your unmai as our arms. Warriors   *truth*
of the Tolkaapiyam on Galle Face Green
paying with our blood for your right to be.
Oru naadillaathe aatkal, in exile,   *A people without a country*
bearing the music of your beauty, still.

The Sinhala Only Act (1956) demoted Tamil from being one of the national
languages of Sri Lanka. The Act was met with widespread protests. The law was
repealed a few years later.

The *Tolkaapiyam*: This is the earliest written Tamil Grammar, believed to have
originated, in written form from oral sources, sometime between 10BC and 5BC.
This text is a fundamental cornerstone of Tamil literature.

முகமூடி செய்பவள்

by Vinothini

அவளது வீட்டின் சுவர்களெங்கும்
அவள் செய்யும் முகங்கள்.

தனது
குருதியிலொரு துளி
மூச்சின் ஒற்றைத் துணுக்கு
மூப்புறுந் தசைத்திரள் சிறிது சேர்த்து
முகங்கள் செய்கிறாள்.

நடு நிசியில் பகலின் வெளிச்சத்தில்
எனது ஊரில்
எங்கோ ஒரு உயிர் இறக்கையிலும்
மற்றொன்று பிறக்கையிலும்
யாரோ ஒருவர் கொல்லப்படுகையில்
கேள்வி கேட்கும் உரிமை தொலைத்து
அவர்கள் தலைகள் தாழ்கையில்
அவள் முகங்கள் செய்கிறாள்.

ஒரு பெண்ணின் காதல் மறுக்கப்படுகையில்
அவள் பலவந்தமாக இச்சிக்கப்படும் பொழுதுகளில்
குழந்தைகள் பயந்து அழ மறக்கையில்
வெடிச்சத்தங்கள் பறவைகளின் கூடுகளை உலுப்புகை-
யில்
காரணமேதுமற்றுக் கடத்தப்பட்டவன்
தன் வாழ்வு பற்றி அச்சமுறுகையில்
வீடொன்று ஆளற்றுத் தனிக்கையில்
கிராமமொன்று கைவிடப்படுகையில்
அங்கே நாயொன்று
உணவின்றி அலைந்து உயிர்விடுங் கணத்தில்
பாலுந் தேனுங் குடிக்கும் எமது கடவுளர்
இல்லை எனத் திட்டப்படுகையில்

90

அவள் முகங்கள் செய்கிறாள்.
முகங்களின் மூச்சும்
மூடாத கண்களின் பார்வையும்
குழந்தைகளது என ஏமாந்து
அவள் உயிரூட்டும் முகங்கள் எப்படியோ
அவளது கனவுகளைக் களவாடிவிடுகின்றன
அவ்வப்போது.

The Mask-Maker

by Vinothini, a translation.

On the walls of her house
are the masks she has made.

Using a drop of her own blood, a wisp
of her breath, fragments of her aging
muscles, she makes her masks.

Whether in the middle of the night
or at the break of first light,
wherever there is a life waning
or another beginning,
when someone is being oppressed
or another being murdered,
she makes her masks.

During the heartbreak of a love affair
or when a girl is assaulted
when children forget how to cry in fright
when explosions rattle the nests of birds
when a man, disappeared, fears for his life
when a house is abandoned and a village deserted
when a stray dog dies of starvation
when people realise that their gods
having drunk milk and honey
have forsaken them – during these moments,
she makes her masks.

Deceived into thinking that the lifeless masks
with their unseeing, ever open eyes
are like children, she gives them life.
And from time to time they steal her dreams.

Daha Ata Sanniya

Sinhalese: Dance of the Demons
In response to Vinothini 'The Mask-Maker'

August 2018. A set of stamps released
by the Ministry of Posts, celebrating
the sanni yakuma ritual. A Sinhala
folk practice, an exorcism rite; masks
and dancers banishing demons of diseases
back to the underworld.

From folk medicine to dance form, each demon
wears a grotesquely colourful mask.
Eighteen demons on eighteen stamps for eighteen diseases.
The Dewa Sanniya for cholera and typhoid.
The Pith Sanniya, its mask yellow with bilious complaints.
The demon of temporary blindness (a one-eyed mask).
The Gulma Sanniya, the demon of parasitic worms.

Stamp #12 is different. No mask,
just the face of a man: dark skinned,
wide eyed, frenzied. Bare chested
with vibhuti on his forehead.
A grimacing mouth stained red.
The Demala Sanniya, the Demon of Tamil.

Here was the illness plaguing the polity.
In Stamp Bulletin 915 Professor Bentarage
describes this demon as 'craziness, madness,
gibberish. Running here and there. Furrowing
of the forehead; blackening of the face.
Talking in Tamil.'

The Naming of Names 11

Vadivel	Vairavamurthy	Vaithilingam	Vallipuram
Vanathi	Vanithasan	Vanniyasingam	Varatharasa
Varithamby	Varnalingam	Vasagan	Vasanthakumar
Vasanthy	Vaseegara	Vasikala	Veelapoodi
Veen	Veerapandiyan	Veerasingam	Velayutham
Vellaiyan	Velumayilum	Vellupillai	Venkadasamy
Venugopal	Venukaran	Venurajah	Venuthas
Varatheeswaran	Veerasegaram	Vetrivel	Vikunthavasan
Vijayabavan	Vijayalingam	Vijayaluxsumy	Vijayapalan
Vijayathas	Vijitha	Vikanthan	Vikneswaran
Vilvaraja	Vimala	Vimalanathan	Vinasithamby
Vinoraja	Vinosan	Vinothakumar	Vinotharan
Vinothini	Vipulananthar	Visittamma	Visumappoodi
Visvalingam	Visvanathan	Visvaranjan	Vithushan
Vivekananthan	Yogamalar	Yogan	Yogananthan
Yogaraja	Yogeswary	Yokanatha	Yugamini
Yuvani			

Alagaiah	Alagaratnam	Ampigapathy	Ananthasamy
Appathurai	Arudselvan	Arulpragasam	Arulthas
Balasingham	Gnanasegaram	Gunaratnam	Gunaseelan
Inthiranath	Jeevaratnam	Jeyanthimalar	Jeyarani
Jeyaveeran	Kajenthiran	Kalathevi	Kamalan
Kamalanayaki	Kanagan	Kanagaratnam	Kanniah
Kapilraja	Ketharan	Kirubairasa	Krishnapillai
Kuberan	Kumarathasan	Lakshmi	Lalith
Mahenthiran	Malar	Malliga	Mohanasuntharam
Murugupillai	Muththan	Muthusami	Nagamuthu
Nagaratnam	Nanthasiri	Navamani	Nesan
Nirmala	Nirmalanathan	… …	… … … …

Things Happen

When they pepper neighbourhoods with imported
mortars and expansive tank fire. When they
go from house to house lining up girls, women
and men in revenge or on a whim –

When they shut down substations and impose
curfews and travel embargoes so that
market sellers face ruin. When people go
unfed, unwashed and scavenge for scraps –

When they shoot blindfolded men in the back
and take souvenirs of mutilated lives
and hopes. When they rape girls and grandmothers
and celebrate the hecatomb of their success –

things happen
and the world moves on.

Easter Bombings, 2019

Who now remembers Anita,
Alex and Annabel Nicolson?
Bill Harrop and his wife Sally Bradley?
Lorraine Campbell, known as Loz?

They had strayed into another country's
bloody story, and for a few days
they were the catch in our breath,
the missed beat of our hearts.

But according to Google, more people
searched for Notre Dame after the fire,
than they did the Easter Bombings,
and as a country we quietly forgot.

Now April 21st only holds significance
to those they left behind.

Epitaph on a Tyrant
after W H Auden

He is the man you should never invite to dinner.
For his appetite is monstrous – craving legs,
arms, teeth and bones. Sucks them into the pit
of his mouth and spits out the gristle, an odd button,
the remnant of a shirt. Grieving families hang around
his table waiting for these projectiles. Scramble
to see whether this time, this time
there was something to reclaim, to place in the ground.

He is the man you should never share a joke with.
For behind his laughter is the roar of a gunship.
Each guffaw a depth charge, each giggle
the shriek of a missile. Each time he grins
villages disappear, forests shed their leaves.
He levels mountain tops with a smile
and when he chuckles, fire rains from the sky.

He is not a man you should ever criticise.
For he pays back every syllable with a thousand
deaths. Every line with tears squeezed from the eyes
of children. He can transform commas and semi-colons
into nooses; full-stops and exclamation marks
into gravestones. He is poison, poison, corroding the streets
of a land abandoned by songbirds. And he swallows
the red earth of Jaffna for dessert.

My Grandfather's House

There is moss growing in the bedrooms
of my grandfather's house.
Green and sticky, staining the walls
and the floor with shades of the sea.
They climb, tracing intricate patterns, around
browned squares, where pictures used to hang.

The roof has fallen in. Water stagnates
on a cushioned floor as disturbed bats circle,
drawing the night in. The rooms are empty
of all that was him. The doors have been locked
warped and unwilling to open onto
a tomorrow which does not contain him.

It is six o'clock and the mosquitos
gather noisily in rooms that once
smelt of sweet margossa leaves.
They are the music makers, the sum total
of our dreams. The inheritors of rooms
that reek and sweat in angry dismay.

There is moss growing in the bedrooms
of my grandfather's house and raindrops
sing a lament on deserted floors.

Colombo, May 9 2022
(The burning of Mahinda Rajapaksa's House)

As you cram papers, cash, clothes hurriedly
into bags, do you feel the breath constrict
in your throat? Are you sweating, panicking?
Are you? Are you?

They are watching you.
The mother who starved with her baby
on the road to Mullivaikkal.
Men with chests opened by your bullets.
Children whose terror you ignored.
They have crowded into every corner
of the room from floor to ceiling,
and look – there are thousands more clamouring
to get in. Can you see them?

On the street outside, a woman –
one of your people – is screaming in Sinhala
that she will hang you from a lamppost
by your prick. Can you hear her?
What passions you do arouse in people.
Look. There goes your house in flames.
Do you see it? It burns just as mine did,
and his, and theirs, and hers.

To Name their Names

Abinaya	*laughter, happiness. A gift from God.*
Adaikalam	*a refuge*
Amirthanayagi	*a girl with eternal life*
Anatharatnam	*gemlike, brimming with joy*
Anpalagan	*the beautiful, beloved one*
Chinnan	*little one*
Ilanthiraiyan	*an energetic man whose influence will extend beyond the sea*
Inpamalar	*the flower of happiness*
Ithayashanthini	*a heart filled with peace*
Jalini	*one who is held up by water*
Jayatha	*the giver of happiness*
Jeban	*a man called to prayer*
Jeevakumar	*a child brimming with life*
Jeyapriya	*a lover of victory*
Kalarani	*Queen of the arts*
Kanatheepan	*a legendary archer*
Kanmani	*pearl of our eyes*
Karunakaran	*one cradling an ocean of compassion*
Kodiyarasan	*fierce, like a warrior king*
Kokila	*a nightingale*
Kularatnam	*jewel of the family*
Lalithathevi	*filled with beauty*
Lavanya	*she with a fighting spirit*
Mangalesvari	*the visionary one*
Manjula	*a spring, brimming with melody*
Manuval	*one born to rule the world*
Meiyan	*one possessing all truth*
Mudiappan	*the one without end*
Myuran	*one who rides a peacock*
Nanthini	*daughter*

Narayanapillai	*the child of the eternal man*
Narmathan	*a blessing to the world*
Nesarani	*Queen of kindness*
Nithianantham	*one filled with eternal bliss*
Ponniah	*the golden man*
Rajini	*a beautiful, dark night*
Rathimalar	*a flower of desire*
Rohan	*one who is free*
Sanjeevan	*one who will achieve immortality*
Santhosam	*one filled with happiness*
Sathananthakumar	*a son of perpetual happiness*
Shakuntala	*a songbird*
Subakaran	*one who does good*
Sumathy	*bearer of peace*
Thannimalai	*a waterfall*
Thanusiya	*a gift from God*
Thusyanthy	*life's most cherished one*
Varathan	*a blessing*

Based on the important work carried out by the North East Secretariat on Human Rights (NESHR) in Sri Lanka, who catalogued each massacre of the civilian population during the civil war, producing a brief description, a map and eye witness accounts (where existing). Each report ended with a list of names of those killed. Sometimes there were only a few names, sometimes there were hundreds. Sometimes, where entire villages had been wiped out, no names were recorded. Without their methodical cataloguing of the names of the dead, often in dangerous conditions, I would not have been able to write this book. I have only been able to use a small sample of all the names I collected. These in turn are but a small sample of all the names that were lost over twenty-six years.

Acknowledgements

With thanks to the editors of the following magazines and anthologies in which versions of some of these poems were first published: *Modern Poetry in Translation; Out of Sri Lanka: Tamil, Sinhala and English Poetry from Sri Lanka and its Diasporas; The North; POETRY; London Grip; Reliquiae Journal; The Interpreter's House; Centres of Cataclysm: 50 Years of Modern Poetry in Translation; The Gutter Magazine; Poetry London.* My thanks also to Ilkley Literature Festival and Manasamitra for commissioning some of the poems appearing here. 'Muthumai Kolam' was one of the winners of the *Silenced Shadows* competition, run by Amnesty International.

My sincere thanks go to Ann and Peter Sansom at whose writing workshops many of these poems were born. To Peter who, with care and reassurance, steered this book to publication. To the staff at The Poetry Business, especially Keith Lauchlan for laying out my words so beautifully, and Pete Hebden for ushering this book into the outside world. To Vidyan Ravinthiran and Sylee Gore who read and commented on early drafts of the book; to the members of The Collective who were often the first readers of many of these poems; to Anthony Ezekiel Capildeo and Clare Pollard for their kind support of the book.

Thank you Kinara Poets (Gita Ralleigh, Anita Pati, Rushika Wick, Sarala Estruch and Sylee Gore) for your fellowship. Thank you Happy Hookers (Alex, Ann, Claire, Emma, Kate, Kate, Kirsty & Liyana) for your love and friendship.

To Richard, Kit and Becky – you are my hearthstones, the persistent beat of my heart.